Scribblings of a Sca

The Second Wave

POETRY BY DIANNE TRAYNOR

I sit on my porch
And talk to the moon
Words hang like cobwebs
My pen is my broom

Strategic Book Publishing and Rights Co.

Strategic Book Publishing and Rights Co., LLC
USA | Singapore
www.sbpra.net

For information about special discounts for bulk purchases, please contact Strategic Book Publishing and Rights Co. Special Sales, at bookorder@sbpra.net.

ISBN: 978-1-68235-324-0

Book Design: Suzanne Kelly

With love and gratitude

To the beautiful souls who:

trust me with their innermost thoughts,

gift me their inspiring photography,

feel a connection with my words,

and travel this road with me.

For my daughter, Bianca,

and my mother, Cecile.

My love always

Table of Contents

I think 3

A drive to nowhere 5

Euphoria...7

Lean on me 9

Pain pays forward too 11

Booyah..13

Sweet sleep 15

Ethereal Love..16

Fire fades; rivers flow..19

Questions...21

Magic waits...23

Cowboy in my Scotch..25

Tonight I feel...27

True happiness 29

A morning note to Moby 31

Hello..32

Puppet master...35

Come sail with me 37

She hunts...39

Craved captivity 41

Words will never be enough 42

There comes a time...47

Geronimo 49

Nature's high...51

Higher ground 53

Desire begs surrender 55

Kiss me 57

Dance with the devil 59

Unexpected delights..61

Deep sleep calling...63

Cathedral bells 64

How strange 67

Home..69

Lost in the shadows of love 71

A life lived 72

One step 75

Autumn leaves 77

Dear lover 79

Braveheart..81

Truth—Belief—Love..83

Our love 85

Only in dreams...87

Beauty in the madness 88

The fire still burns..90

How do I love thee 93

Warrior heart..94

Awakening to a new world 97

All the while 101

Rickety Caboose 102

Destination unknown 105

Seasons...106

Sketchpad...109

Free to choose 110

A Moby moment 112

A poet's verse...115

A note of thanks 117

Scribblings of a Scattered Mind

The Second Wave

Author, Dianne Traynor, lives in Melbourne Australia where they had one of the longest, and strictest, Covid-19 Lockdowns of anywhere in the world.

It was during their second wave that this collection came to be.

I THINK

I think
That it's time
To think no more
An old worn-out song
Where it all went wrong
Time I closed that door.

I've prayed
And I've wept
For what could have been
Worked too many years
Not for love, but for bills
Now I think "how obscene!".

I've wished
For a love
That I have not found
I've felt pain
Embraced sorrow
And darkness profound.

So, every day now
I make sure that I laugh
As it's all quite absurd
Simply closing my eyes
And opening my mind
To a future preferred.

For now, I'm alone
Just me on my own
New dream in my hand
And I think
I'll just feel
My feet in the sand.

A DRIVE TO NOWHERE

Do you have an open heart
The courage to let go
Of times and words that do not serve
The future seeds you've yet to sew?

You know the sun is shining here
Rain glistens quietly upon the grass
I feel you sitting on my porch
Embracing the warmth of memories past

Your eyes so dark and deep I see
Your voice just lilts so near
Reverberating through my soul
Our secret moments crystal clear

I make, nor need, false promise
I've learned I'm not afraid
To be alone, hold onto hope
And dream of what remains

So, would you take a drive to nowhere?
Perhaps you will come by

EUPHORIA

She drank him in as he drank wine;

the level of euphoria as addictive

as any substance she had ever known.

He played her heartstrings as masterfully

as he played the guitar,

and she would willingly listen to his music

for the rest of her days.

LEAN ON ME

I am the power
that opens your eyes
to face a new day

I am the flower
that opens your mind
to bring joy to your heart

I am the shower
in the gentle rain
that washes away your tears

I am the tower
of strength
that helps you overcome

I am love
I am everywhere
and I wait

Do not fear me lost
I am always here
Lean on me

© Mark Starr

10

PAIN PAYS FORWARD TOO

Oh lover, why must I miss you?
My racing heart, my beaded skin,
that you got under and nestled in

I wonder, where are you now?
Whose heart beats in time with yours
in my place, in your arms?

My love, why is it that I cannot forget
your face, your touch?
Haunting me day and night

I ask you, am I forgotten?
Only a distant memory of a fleeting moment
in your timeline of women

Can you tell me why you broke in
just to feed me false hope, turn my heart inside out,
infest my mind and leave?

Oh lover, what woman
scorned you so badly that you now pay forward
a broken heart in vengeance?

Please tell me, will time heal me?
Set me free to love another?
Or am I a wheel in the cycle of scorn?

For in innocence,
pain pays forward too

BOOYAH!

You try too hard to make it right
Just stop your fuss and do not fight
Now throw your arms up in the air
And shout it out: "I just don't care!"

So, bring that smile
Upon your dial
There is no need to frown

Or to keep yourself surrounded
by a bunch of freakin' clowns!

Booyah!

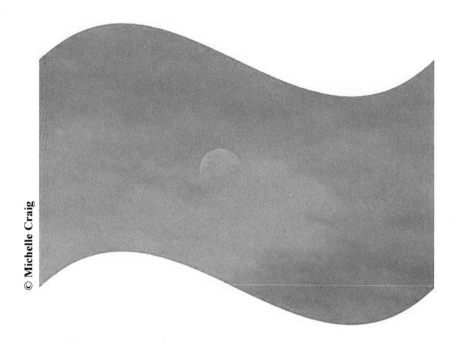

SWEET SLEEP

Oh, Sleep

Sweet Sleep

Won't you visit?

Won't you stay a while?

I miss you

ETHEREAL LOVE

My love

Every day of my life
I have felt you,
and yet you are not here;
just a revolving door of imposters.

You know

I have been loved for my looks,
a pretty accessory,
but it did not last;
there is always one prettier.

I have been loved for my body,
when it was sleek and finely tuned,
but it did not last;
there is always one sleeker.

I have been loved for my house by the bay,
beautifully renovated at my hand,
but it did not last;
once sold, they moved on.

I have been loved for my position,
considered by others of importance,
but it did not last;
there is always one more important.

I have been loved for my sense of humour,
the ability to drag another from darkness,
but it did not last;
there is always one lighter.

I have been loved for my mind,
my determination to help another succeed,
but it did not last;
once successful, they departed.

And I too have been guilty
of being entranced by looks, power and status,
but it was never going to last;
because they were not you.

Oh, my love

How I ache to see you,
touch you,
make love with you,
please come home . . .

. . . the side door is open.

© Terry Davis

17

FIRES FADE; RIVERS FLOW

The rush and overflow
comes when you are needy,
when you are not whole,
not one with yourself

You grasp and grab,
imagine and glorify,
in vain attempts
to fill the gaping wounds

Pushing, pulling, overwhelming another
provides but a temporary fix,
for your fire fades
or your partner burns

When the self is full
there is no rush,
no aching need to hold,
just a peaceful surrender

Learn from the river, watch how it runs,
slowly, quickly, over rocks, sand and stone,
never stopped by question, never halted by doubt,
complete in its journey, insistent, alone

Simply,
surely,
naturally,
with purpose,
the river returns to source.

QUESTIONS

She was just a girl
living in a strange, strange world,
hoping for true love,
but no longer trusting
in its existence

There were lots all around
who would talk, making sounds,
not actually saying
anything
of substance

You will find her day after day
sitting alone, at her sidewalk cafe,
pen lovingly held,
scribbled pages before her,
mind miles away

Asking questions her writing may answer

MAGIC WAITS

With bended brow you saw her,
lapping waves pushing her your way,
you listened and you heard
her heart calling

Gently, you opened the palm of your hand,
taking her and whispering what she wanted to hear,
you waited, watched and anticipated
as she nervously opened herself to you

Like a flighty fish, strange creature that you are,
distracted by shiny hooks aplenty,
avoiding capture, you kept swimming,
circling and hiding from her substance

Like a lover in a fishmonger's stall,
you traded her as they did wares,
soon she found herself washed upon the shore,
empty, waiting and wanting

Sensuality proving her dominance,
you shattered and scattered the dreams of the innocent,
but at least in her innocence she had dared to risk,
finding magic and colour amidst the dangerous depths

Wetting only your toes, you collect your average little shells,
discarding the unusual that may arouse you to question,
quickly tossing them back into the deep blue seas,
where they cannot be heard nor seen

True of heart she believes,
that as the earth turns and day breaks,
and as the sun shines through the ocean tablet,
a star will rise through the deep waters to the blue skies

and lonely broken hearts will mend it its light

COWBOY IN MY SCOTCH

How is it the sun can shine
yet we can be cold to the bone?

How is it that people with heart
sit in thought drinking alone?

How many cigarettes does it take
to see a dream in the smoke?

Is there a truth in the liquor
for the sad and lonely folk?

Is the answer right there
if you take another swig?

Is the image before you
just your mind playing tricks?

Perhaps winter is leaving
turning grey skies to blue

Or is the field still all muddy
and you have a hole in your shoe?

Perhaps there is a cowboy on a trusty steed
about to blaze in and save you from you
Strong arm round your waist, he throws you aboard,
Ooops, straight on over and face down in poo!

Oh, waiter,
Dear waiter
Please bring me another scotch
With a side order of cigars

Oh hell,
just bring me the bottle!

© Dianne Traynor

26

TONIGHT I FEEL

Tonight,
I feel you out there
somewhere

and I want

to feel the blood rush to my cheeks when you tell me I am
beautiful because you see more than others see

to feel the anticipation as your fingers brush against my hand,
wondering whether you will take it in yours, cupped or fingers
entwined

to feel the energy racing through my body as I lose myself to
imaginings of possibility, dreams and future moments

to feel the desire to stay awake just to watch you as my eyelids
too heavy to remain open, close and I drift into a world of
peace

to feel the excitement when the telephone rings and I hear your
voice, waiting for my heart to slow down that I may hear your
words

to feel the sensations, share the laughter, ride the rollercoaster,
bask in your eyes and sail in the intimacy of trust

to feel nervousness and shyness do battle with temptation and
lust, surrendering to the loss of reality and drift to the island
that only we inhabit

to feel
to simply feel
your love

If only I knew who you were

TRUE HAPPINESS

True happiness—for me

    is that moment when I am outside myself looking in,

    hearing every single rustle of a leaf,

    every scratch of the pen against the paper,

    seeing every colour a little richer

    and feeling every pore of my skin in touch with the breeze.

In that moment,

    I feel connected

    with everything

    and everyone that I love.

It is fleeting,

    and it is my daily dream and endeavour

    to live more in that moment.

30

A MORNING NOTE TO MOBY

The ferns are rustling
A crow squawks somewhere in the distance
Chirpy birds scurry in flight past the verandah
And my eyes stare at this page
As if I look long enough you will appear
Hands cold, wanting to be held in yours
Thoughts scattered in play
I would swear there's a hole in my stomach from missing you
But I know this is ridiculous
Yet it is how it feels

The birds seem to get louder
More joining in the chorus
Snorting puppy as accompaniment
As if nature is making a musical comedy of my solitude
Glancing at my phone
There's always the temptation
To replay your message
That makes me smile just to hear your voice
Wanting it to beep, wanting it to ring
It sits silently upon the table
As if mocking me

I'll just have another cigarette
And sit quietly
Letting the breeze caress my face and rub my shoulders
In your absence
A sip of fresh coffee
To warm the inner space
Watching the birds hippity hop
On the neighbour's shade cloth
And dream
I'm in your arms

HELLO

Standing at the pedestrian crossing,
she felt a young girl inside her body,
looking into a shop window reflection
she saw someone else before her
and she desperately wanted to say hello.

She is someone who has questioned herself for a lifetime,
someone who always felt less than,
someone who seemed to feel differently,
someone who would feel lost at home
and at home when lost.

Her selfish self still mourns
for the close family, the loving husband, the home by the sea
    and the successful career,
for the world so alien to her own.
She wonders when exactly the rails broke
and she fell into the water tumbling toward today.

But the girl, the girl still breathing deep within her
whispers to let her know
she is exactly who she was meant to be,
finally doing what she was born to do
and living where she will one day be grateful she found herself.

Free from the need for bigger, brighter and shinier,
appreciating beauty in simple form,
accepting change and embracing what is,
the girl knows she is taking steps to free herself
from the shadows of others, ceasing the futile comparisons.

Skipping through her soul, across her heart,
sending vibrations of youthful promise,
the girl reminds her that although there are no guarantees,
if she continues to believe and dream
tomorrow may bring unimaginable beauty.

The girl knows
the painting is not finished,
the portrait is only partially sketched,
the music is only half written,
and the dance is a long way from over.

As she looked again, the words hung before her
waiting patiently to be picked
Excitedly they circled her with love,
for every day they wanted to play with her
and at long last . . .

She felt them,
saw them,
smiled at them,
held them warmly in her hand
and paid them forward.

Standing at the pedestrian crossing,
she felt a young girl inside her body,
looking into a shop window reflection
she saw herself before her
and she happily said hello.

© Dianne Traynor

33

© David Christian

PUPPET MASTER

Poor Puppet,
fell in love with the Puppet Master
in a field of dreams and promises.

Puppet Masters know not how to love,
they break the lock
not hold the key.

Oh, puppet, you do not belong
in that sad and sorry box
where he thought he could keep you.

Beautiful and scattered, remember
you are the flower, loving in purity;
he is the weed, strangling beauty.

Shading hope from sunlight,
he is a Thief of Hearts
travelling in darkness.

Abandon his game of tug,
break free of his control
and relish your freedom.

Oh, puppet, darling puppet,
he was never worthy.
Puppet Masters rarely are.

COME SAIL WITH ME

If your leg is weary,
lean on me
If your load too heavy,
let me share the burden
If your head is hurting,
lay it on my shoulder
If you are full of excitement,
dance with me
If your heart aches,
I will listen quietly until its rhythm returns

And should you suffer,
no longer feeling of value,
I will remind you
that your pain will turn to beauty too

Like boats upon the sea,
we shall navigate together
through the storms,
resting in the bay,
each other's buoy when drowning,
each other's fireworks when it's time to rejoice,
surrendering to the absolute depths of love
as we sail into unknown waters,
guided by the light of possibility
and promise.

SHE HUNTS

Bored with your lack of compassion,
your selfishness and falsity,
she walks amidst nature
becoming one with the earth
and snarls,
hunting for freedom
from your empty words.

Angry at your meaningless questions,
the arrogance with which you pretend to care,
she pounds the stones
discarding the notion that truth
could ever come from your lips,
and she spends her days contemplating
reasons to not rip your throat out.

Seething at feigned concern,
your empty heart poisoning her soul,
she leaves the pack
to travel alone
far away,
searching for a new home
from all that abandoned her.

She hunts,
bleeding and dying inside,
refusing to surrender
she stands proud,
her spirit magnificent in its tenacity
and she will, despite you,
survive!

CRAVED CAPTIVITY

Did he not know that she had devoured his words with such thirst?

Some would cry entrapment

but it was the captivity she craved

in the freedom of his mind.

WORDS WILL NEVER BE ENOUGH

Skin
paper thin
like tissue
wrapping a body
once strong
now fragile

Bones
crumbling
like the sphinx
testimony
to the years
of hardship and toil

Eyes
once bright
pool with tears
as pain strikes
yet another blow
to an already exhausted body

Mind
always sharp
now clouded
with morphine
a vain attempt
at relief

Will
once powerful
unstoppable
now surrendering
in a desire
for peace

Heart
so big and bright
fades
into a tiny frame
suffering
interminable pain

Life
a harsh mistress
to let you suffer
excruciatingly
after years of sacrifice
for so many

My dearest mother
may the beat of my heart
the warmth of my hand
the depth of my love
bring comfort
in this your darkest hour

44

Selfishly,
So very selfishly,
I do not want to say goodbye.
Lovingly,
if you want to go,
I will

Mother,
remember the field
where father waits patiently
to take your hand
and live the stolen years
of your love

Three little words . . .
"I love you"
will never be enough

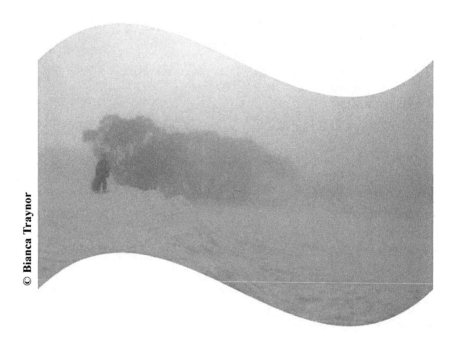

THERE COMES A TIME

There comes a time
when you must disassociate yourself
from all you have known,
perhaps believed,
because to remain
will drag you deeper into darkness,
blood turning black with poison
of disappointment and anger
at those you cannot change.

There comes a time
when you must open your heart
to your loneliness,
brace and embrace yourself,
take your own hand,
walk away in the frightening knowledge
that you are on your own,
alone,
waiting only on the will of tomorrow.

There comes a time
when you find yourself teetering
on the edge of the abyss,
one foot ready to leap,
one holding you back,
and you must decide
if the sunshine
and the moon
are enough.

There comes a time,
and that time
is now.

GERONIMO

Hooked
Wriggle wriggle
No getting loose

Like a virus with shoes
Running free, roaming wild
No escape, no excuse

Shake, rattle 'n roll
Ah . . . Jiggy jiggy dance
No stopping the music

It's a mystery, that it is
It's a gamble, what's the odds?
Lover boy, are you lucid?

No, no, no
Know, know, know
Is it love?

No way of knowing
No way to tell
If you jump, will you fall?

Fly? Or splat?
Freedom? Or trapped?
Oh, what the hell . . .

Geronimo!

50

NATURE'S HIGH

Breath
Tingle
Nostrils
PULSE
Ache
Echo
Clench
PULSE
Ringing
Ribs
Expand
PULSE
Soft
Lips
Toes
PULSE
Earlobes
Stretch
Wet
PULSE
Hips
Melt
Mould
PULSE
Engulfed
Moist
Eyes
PULSE
Deep
White
Pure
PULSE
Pulse
Pulse
Pulse
HIGH

52

HIGHER GROUND

A last strike
of criticism
became the hand
to break through
rose-coloured glasses
worn too long
shattering illusions

Harsh and cutting words
sliced through invisible bonds
around the heart
freeing a soul once lost
to false hope
lifting
a veil of pretence

A dream spent
on unrequited love,
a goodbye
feared and resisted
gave way
to a strange sense of calm
and new strength

Love given unconditionally
taken for granted, or abused,
will eventually seek a new beginning,
either the old lover learns
and changes,
or love moves
to higher ground

DESIRE BEGS SURRENDER

A body yearns
New knowledge learned
Distant bells are ringing

Mind talking
Fearful heart baulking
You cannot stop the dance

Quiet truth hears your call
Barriers commanded, fall
And light does flicker on the hill

In timeless dreams, a stranger comes
Desire wets a waiting hungry tongue
Begging you surrender

Slumbered passion shadily awakes unafraid
Revealing paths not walked, unplanned, unmade
Erotic silence whispers, "Ssshhh . . . Be Still"

He sees you

56

KISS ME

Kiss me
As if you are James Bond
And the very passion in your lips
Will save the world

Kiss me
As if you are Batman
And the breathlessness that I may feel
Will conquer evil

Kiss me
As if you are Spiderman
And the web that binds us
Will eradicate a madman's plan

Kiss me
As if you are Iron Man
And the heat that passes between us
Will melt the cold hearts of humanity

Kiss me
As if I am the answer to all problems
And the passage between worlds
Will feel as effortless as the breeze

Kiss me
As if this is our last moment on this mortal plane
And the energy with which you flame my desire
Will bring eternal peace and love

So, kiss me darling
For in those lips I am immortal

DANCE WITH THE DEVIL

What a sweet melody
You hear as he sings
When you want to believe

What a rhythm you feel
At the beat of his hand
When you want to believe

What a tingling runs through
Sliding into dark eyes
When you want to believe

And the voice of reason goes unheard
Silenced by loneliness
When you want to believe

So tonight
You surrender
Because you want to believe

But you know, yes you know
As you drip in the dream
That it's all make-believe

Disregarding tomorrow
Due to too many nights
On your own, all alone

Now it's time
To dance with the devil
As he whispers your name

UNEXPECTED DELIGHTS

It need not always be the perfect garden
for the beautiful to spring forth
and surprise you
bringing a smile to your day.

Take delight in those unexpected moments
that are gifted to you
keep your eyes, mind and heart
open.

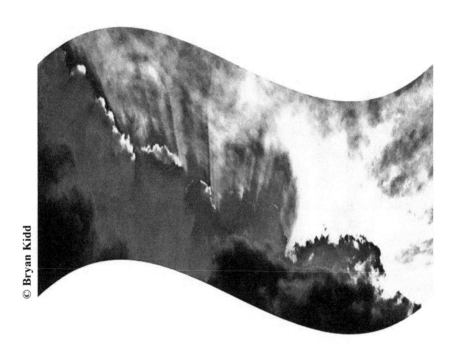

© Bryan Kidd

DEEP SLEEP CALLING

Rusty
My wheels have faltered
Reality moving further away,
yet thunderously present

Tempting
One step, she calls me
Open-armed abyss inviting
me to slide through the heavens

Tears
Like a waterfall's caress
Are not felt upon my numb cheeks
whilst the bells take residence in my ears

Sharply awoken
By ghosts of my past
From the deep, dark sleep
that cocooned me for but a moment

White mare in the meadow
Black stallion on the hill
And I stand in the middle,
unheard

Wishing those that I have known
may understand
My intents were always honourable
in a world in which I did not fit

As the night turns
And the seas swell
The clouds gather
to watch the clock strike three times

CATHEDRAL BELLS

The first time I saw your picture
I had to look again,
drawn to you
with such a mixture
of emotions

The first time that we shared words
my mind raced
in anticipation,
as nervousness and hope
became blurred

The first time we met
I had to look away,
not wanting you to see
me blushing
more than I could possibly remember

The first time you stole a kiss
I froze,
not realising the depth
of what I had missed
waiting to meet you

The first time I lay in your arms
would become
a treasured memory
that comes to visit me
in dreams

The first time you took me to the light,
how magical
an adventure
into unknown lands,
the Holy Grail to my heart

The first time you said goodbye
oh, how I wept,
stung by all that was lost,
no matter how I tried
I could not forget you

Now, every time I think of you
and every time I feel my lips meet yours,
no matter how distanced or hopeless,
I return to that place,
that first time

And the bells ring
like a cathedral
on Easter Sunday

HOW STRANGE

How strange of you to think you know me,
when you have spent no time with me,
nor spoken

How strange of you to think you know me,
when you have only seen
what I have chosen for you to see

How strange of you to think you know me,
when you never visit
and I think of how much I have changed

How strange of you to think you know me,
when you never ask of my life
or my dreams

How strange of you to think you know me,
do tell me my favourite movie, writer, pastime or poet,
my greatest achievement and my greatest loss to date

Oh, you cannot?
How odd! So, I wonder why
I find it strange you think you know me

© Graeme Sinclair

HOME

I have spent my entire life looking for "home"
Searching for places, or people, to bring warmth
Making me a gypsy of cities and love

The futility of it all astounds me
For no matter where, or with whom, I found myself
It had all been a pointless endeavour

So many years passing in a sea of emptiness
Because I did not understand, I was already there
I had only to open the door to my words

Wherever I put up house, or in whose arms I lay
If I do not write, I am lost
But if I do—ah, if I do—the sun shines from within

The words can be sombre or joyful, it matters not
For they travel through my heart to paper
To bring me safely home

Teach your children to read and write,
to excel at mathematics, or science, if you will
But also do them the biggest favour of all

Encourage them early to find their passion
That they may grow in strength and be warm when alone
Never feeling the hole within that they do not know how to mend

In the shifting sands of a world that can be cruel,
gift your children an inner impenetrable castle
and they will always be "home"

LOST IN THE SHADOWS OF LOVE

New love cannot claim a heart
whilst the heart remains haunted,
beating for a love that does not dwell in reality

New love cannot excite a body
whilst a ghost sleeps by your side,
the shiver of loss sitting heavy like an impenetrable wall

Love ghosts speak falsely,
and whilst you live in a world of imagined promise,
all others will fade achingly into empty words

The cost of a ghost is high,
the cuts etch deeper by the hour, keeping you weak
whilst blood runs ruby red from a wound that will not heal

Ghosts lurk deeply muddying your mind,
quenching their thirst with your tears
and feeding from your bleeding heart

Ghosts keep lovers lost
in the shadows of a love that is not real,
silencing the part of them that knows

True love lives in warmth and sunshine
even when it is cold
and raining

A LIFE LIVED

A soul took a road
not knowing why,
laying lost in the ward.
Would you live? Would you die?
Then came the darkness,
Black Dog, you did call him,
and the memories they flooded,
of a past they called Sin

Pressure had built
in the heart, in the mind,
till the body could not hold
anymore, deep inside.
Afraid of your own judgement,
you chose many wrong paths,
the years that continued
left you fragile, like glass

So many moments
of errors in time,
but it's never too late
for a new life to find.
You don't sleep much I know,
your thoughts never stop,
and time seems so fleeting,
stop watching the clock!

Age is only a number
when it comes to your soul,
I ask you remember
you are never too old.
Take your dreams and your hopes,
forget all past blunders,
make it happen, you can,
cast all doubts asunder

Now there's one thing you know,
no matter what else, you did right,
the love shared with your daughter,
the greatest gift of your life.
So, when life gets you down,
think of your girl and feel proud,
you did good, take a bow,
she is beautiful—inside and out!

Now sit by me, sing out to the world,
without care, without doubt,
"I am thankful for the life I have lived
and I will not sell out!"

"There is still so much to share,
your love for life,
and your love for your girl,
is eternal."

© Mark Starr

ONE STEP

One moment
frozen in time

One step
and we can be changed forever

AUTUMN LEAVES

The weather is changing,
there's a cold chill,
leaves drift in puddles
of fallen tears of rain

My mind wanders,
as I listen to autumn leaves,
to words you have written
that feel so familiar

Picturing you in your beret,
cigarette drooping from your lips,
I am hoping that you are well
and not weary from internal struggle

Questions hang, taunting me

How does it come to pass
that we can be more in sync with a stranger
we have never met
than with those we believe we know?

Is anonymity the key to freedom of connection?
Are words the pathway to the hidden self?
Can a poet only reveal his true soul in obscurity?
If only we could all unveil our true self in reality.

A smile eases into my soul
as I think of when next we meet,
may it not be too long between drinks
and banter

Be kind to yourself, my friend,
I miss you.

DEAR LOVER

I didn't stop loving you,
I started loving myself

I didn't stop missing you,
I started respecting myself

I didn't stop yearning for you,
I started valuing myself

And I didn't stop dreaming of you,
I just wanted to be part of your dreams too

BRAVEHEART

Do you ever look
at your photographs,
your scraps of paper,
and wonder what others would think
of this person they assume they know?

Have you ever wished
for someone that felt the beating,
heard the same screams
from a caged soul,
trapped and wanting?

Do you ever tire of the game
and want to just drown in a sea of vodka,
smoke a thousand cigarettes,
surrender to debauched loveless sex,
and just say "Fuck you, world"?

But instead,
you sit alone on a dark porch,
or in a silent room,
and write
bleeding words

Where are you Braveheart
that knows me and
understands my darkness

Why don't you find me
and make me yours?

© Mark Starr

TRUTH—BELIEF—LOVE

My heart just rests upon a cloud
Waiting

It's like it separated from the crowd
Believing

Unspoken truth in what it feels
Trusting

Not knowing why beholden
Guidance

I wonder if you see it there?
I wonder if you really care?

But in the end, it matters not
What matters most remains

Truth—Belief—Love
In that order

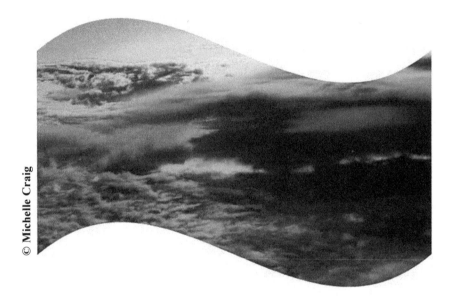

© Michelle Craig

OUR LOVE

Our love will stand firm like the rocks

amidst the shifting sands of life

and will light the skies on fire

ONLY IN DREAMS

Oh, Sweet Dreams, let me surrender
to the gift you bring,
Oh, Sweet Dreams, let me lay in the arms
of your ocean,
rather than in the cold embrace of reality

Oh, Sweet Dreams, let me bask
in your moonlight,
Oh, Sweet Dreams, let me feel the warmth
of the beating heart within you,
rather than the damp absence in reality

Oh, Sweet Dreams, let me play in the sand
with the lover within you,
Oh, Sweet Dreams, let me feel the wonder
in your laughter,
rather than the painful tears of reality

Oh, Sweet Dreams, I wait for you
to come,
Oh, Sweet Dreams, I wish
I could stay a little longer,
rather than return to the bleakness of my reality

Oh, Sweet Dreams, you are the strength
that moves me forward,
Oh, Sweet Dreams, you are the hope
that brings me joy

Oh, Sweet Dreams, I wait for the day
you become my reality

BEAUTY IN THE MADNESS

How could I begin
to explain
what I myself do not understand?
A connection that pulls on the heart,
as if a game of tug,
like a puppy pulling on a rope at play

You may think me quite mad,
the oddity
of it all is so bewildering,
even to me,
as if it was always there,
a knowing laying dormant until we met

The shadows came
to cover the sun
and I wandered lost amidst my thoughts
of what had happened,
as if there were no doorways
from this dark room that I had stumbled into

Oh, how can I begin
to explain
that which I myself do not understand?
So, I shall sit quietly
and believe,
until the doorway opens and the sunshine floods over me

You may think me quite mad,
a dreamer
in a land of harsh reality
Perhaps I am,
for I can see your eyes and hear your voice
in my isolation

All I know is I choose to wait here alone,
eyes closed,
picturing you beside me,
rather than walk amidst aimless encounters,
second-rate versions,
that are not you

Should I even begin
to try to explain,
attempting to understand,
or just accept
what is
and be grateful for the crossing of paths

Perhaps there is a sanity,
an unspoken truth and a beauty
in the madness,
I shall let it course its way through my veins,
like seaweed tumbling in the tides of my dream,
searching for the lost shores of your heart

THE FIRE STILL BURNS

She came last night,
three times.
Breaking free, I ran,
holding my chest
to ease her electrical stabbing.

She stalks me,
every night,
looking for my moment of weakness,
when I will surrender,
wrapping myself in her blanket.

She knows me,
how tired I am.
Patiently she prowls my life,
determined to pull me
from my world to hers.

She lurks in the shadows,
turning pink clouds to grey,
sketching,
whilst I write
my gateway of words.

She rides a black stallion,
his beauty inviting,
magnificently proud.
Her porcelain features
deceivingly beautiful.

She knows I'm not ready,
yet she remains persistently haunting.
Her presence profound,
drinking thirstily
my sorrow.

She watches with pleasure,
my splashes erratic,
colouring canvas
of continuous battle,
painting promise.

She circles
the fires I burn,
waiting for tears
to turn fire to ash,
offering her opening.

Staring her down
though weary as hell,
wounds weeping,
deep breath, my battle mind cries,
"I'm not ready."

The fire still burns!

© Michelle Craig

HOW DO I LOVE THEE?

I love thee in the shadows stretching from my soul to cover
the evening lawn

I love thee in the glow of my dreams shining from the lamps
that guard the empty streets

I love thee in the pulsing of my knowing that turns into a
cricket's song echoing through the night's still air

I love thee with an aching heart that beats in rhythm with your
own, unknowingly

I love thee patiently, quietly, as a stolen promise unspoken

I love thee completely

And when we meet, I pray thee love me in return

WARRIOR HEART

Released, I look back
upon your self-made prison,
wishing I could have helped
bring you freedom

Waves of change
wash away your song,
replacing anger
with pity

Filled with bitterness,
you spread your hurt
like margarine on toast,
causing a body of pain

Feeling despair at your words,
your actions bringing tears,
it was not me you robbed of happiness,
but yourself

Insidious thoughts,
body rotting from within,
you charred your heart
with venom

Coating my soul,
weathering your storm,
I will not cower to your darkness,
nor admire it

Self-made prisons
are dark, cold and lonely,
but in the end
it is your choice to remain there

There are no walls,
only barriers
imposed upon yourself
to scale

It is the Warrior Heart
that holds the key

AWAKENING TO A NEW WORLD

I did not turn out how I was supposed to,
how I was supposed to turn out
I am not sure.
But I am sure
I did not turn out how I was supposed to.
My sister is brilliant
and a high achiever,
my brother too.
Ten years on came the little black sheep,
Baaa baaa and a little unglued.

Always searching for my own identity,
constant comparison edging me
to pursue what was expected.
Won awards, praise and promotions,
that left me empty and unfulfilled.
Trying to find what I loved
always made me feel guilty,
and so,
I would return
to the shoes that did not fit.

The years passed,
relationships failed,
uneasiness
took residence
in my heart.

The day came
when the body rebelled,
temporary paralysis
and loss of memory,
but I still wasn't listening.
Returning to what others saw as normal,
I jumped straight back onto the treadmill,
trying so hard

to be what others expected,
chest constricted and mind faltering.

Sensitive to judgement and criticism,
I continued to try,
my soul all the while
preparing for war against my body.
Soldiering on,
living in a world you do not feel a part of
erodes at your core,
until pieces of you break
floating away
and you stumble and fall.

And then came a shift
I would accept,
then reject,
enter my world, return to theirs
Afraid to be me,
feelings of failure,
embarrassment and shame
to be so different to the others.
No wealth, no glory, no fame,
merely an oddity of existence.

Like a tsunami of awakening
In a time of isolation
I woke up and said "NO", as I am is enough!
Stepping onto a tightrope
over a very deep ravine,
taking one step at a time,
I am holding my own,
believing
the time is now
to simply be who I am.

I'll never be wealthy and I'll never be famous,
and that is okay by me.

I have loved and I have given
in ways many will never know,
never see.
Now I sit here at my desk,
Listening to the birds in the distance, feeling the air on my
    skin.
Aware of the kitten that purrs in my bed, and the thoughts in
    my head,
pen in my hand,
this is me.

You may like me, you may not.
You may judge me.
For the time I have left,
let me tell you,
it will only be my judgement that counts.
My Truth,
My Life.
And I say,
"Good Morning World",
It is so nice to meet you.

Now the one you have known
may have passed in the night,
and the one that lay dormant,
only visited on occasion,
now sits at the table.
Look into my eyes,
take a moment, pause and decide,
stay or leave makes no difference.
Finally—thank God—I am happy alone,
company merely a pleasant interruption.

So, shall I make you a coffee?
Or shall I open the gate?
Whatever you choose
Is okay
For I have already chosen

ALL THE WHILE

She walks alone
with your breath inside her

And she waits
until you call her name

All the while

She keeps a warm heart
where dreams fan memories,
and memories stoke dreams,

and you know.

RICKETY CABOOSE

There are those of us that must accept
we have a wire loose,
I know for one that I am travelling
in a rickety caboose.

Once upon a time
we may have had it all together,
but then our little engines
ran into fierce and stormy weather.

So, through the floor or out the door,
a screw might drop, a bolt might fly.
Squeaky wheels, clanging bars,
drifting smoke, the occasional sigh.

So forward ho, you now must go,
climbing up the hill.
Visiting a pity party, passing right on through,
pick up the pace, fire up the heart, no time for standing still.

Looking through the cracks,
no going back to find the missing screw.
We must learn to ride it out,
embrace the flaws, turn grey to blue.

Now sometimes you will rattle
but onward you must roll,
chugging on to find the field
of other like-minded souls.

There will be times that you will wonder,
why it had to be this way,
but I want you to remember,
that there will come the day . . .

When you will look back and smile
upon this roughshod ride,

knowing you held out a loving hand
to sustain another during their low tide.

Surge forward in your dream,
see flowers on the skyline
Give while you can and while you must
Soon enough, you'll wish there'd been more time.

But when the time draws near,
in gratitude you may cry,
when you realise that the hardship, toil and sacrifice,
were building wings for you to fly.

Those wings will take you places
that others cannot see,
you'll travel light of heart and soul, no need for earthly things,
and then you will come visit me . . .

amidst the flowers in the sky.

© Mark Starr

DESTINATION UNKNOWN

In my mind you breathe
My dream
As real as the food at my table

Sitting quietly in your arms
Squiggling my toes, you hold me
Knowing my pain, you sustain me

Diving into your beautiful body
You surround me and keep me safe
Silencing that which would harm me

Riding your shoulders
Standing on tippy toe
I touch the moon

Ah—my dream

You feed me
Cleanse me
Embody me

SEASONS

You came to me in summer
the sun felt warmer,
the breeze brushed playfully,
the birds sang in harmony,
the air tasted sweeter,
and the nights were starry

We moved into autumn
the sun only came out at times,
the breeze became a little brisker,
the birds began to fly south,
the air became a little thicker,
and the nights a little cooler

You drove me into winter
the sun hid behind the clouds,
the breeze chilled me to the bone,
the birds were nowhere to be seen,
the air was cold and wet,
and the nights were dark

Although you were already gone
Winter would not take its leave.
I remained frozen in time,
season after season passed me by,
feeling like summer
would never hold me again

Many seasons passed
and you did not return.
I lost count of the full moons
that shone down on me
attempting to melt away the pain
and the loss

Just when all seemed hopeless,
a long-awaited spring arrived,
flowers burst out to greet me,
the breeze came back to play,
the birds returned to sing,
and the stars filled the night sky

The heart needs time to heal
It may take many seasons
Let it take the time it needs; it knows best.
It will rest and restore,
emptying and refilling,
until ready to embrace possibility once more

Simply surrender
and believe that summer will return

© Dianne Traynor

108

SKETCHPAD

Can I sketch a new beginning?
Let go the fear that it's too late
Erase the past, blot out mistakes
Of demons I did satiate?

A nick, a tear, mine to repair
A broken crayon in my hand
Blank canvas placed upon the table
Hopes filtered by the shifting sands

I close my eyes, shade out the blue
Draw deep into this battered heart
Aching forth a rainbow palette
See the outline of a brand-new start

Replace old images in my mind
Set down the corners by my name
Breathe, believe and keep the faith
There's time to build a brand-new frame

Picturing my easel by the sea
Scatter thoughts out to the wind
Let them circle, be reborn
Then reel them right back in

Can I sketch a new beginning?
Blur the darkened charcoal
Grasping onto dreams of life and love
And feed this weary soul?

Staring into nothingness
On bended knee I pray
That the future in my mind
Is but an unseen stroke away

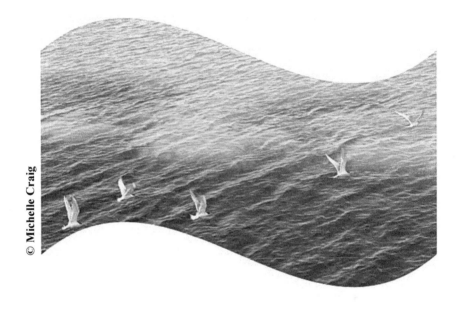

FREE TO CHOOSE

If you do not call for me
I cannot call for you
To do so would only feed your indifference.
In the beginning, how I was warmed
by the longing in your eyes
for only me

Time passed, as did the chase
I did not want to run
In that knowledge your desire turned to apathy.
My heart still yearning and the body still on fire
for only you
I continued to love you in vain

Then the day came when what you saw as a girl walking out
        on you
was really a woman who could no longer bear
to hide from reality.
Being one of many upon whom you call
was not enough for this heart
Still beholden by you, it aches but must go on

Adele says it best when she sings,
"We could have had it all"
It was right there for the taking.
So, if you do not call for me
I cannot call for you
You are set free to choose

May your landing be soft
in a field of happiness
and love

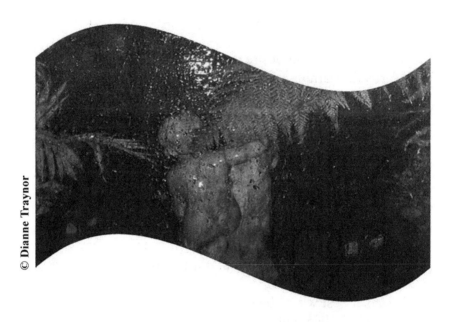

A MOBY MOMENT

A moment
When possibility
Sneaks up on you
Warms you from the inside out
As if you had been standing in the rain
Soaked to the skin
And suddenly you are wrapped in a large fluffy bath towel
In front of a playful vibrant fire
Hands around a delicious cup of hot soup

They say all good things must end
I know not why
The fire dims to scattered charcoal
The towel becomes wet with disappointment
And the chill returns far colder than before
It was only a moment
Yet a defining one
That raises the bar even higher
And your soul cries for the loss of what may have been

© Dianne Traynor

114

A POET'S VERSE

A thousand words left unsaid
A thousand thoughts scatter
like mignonettes into the curtains
drawn against what may have been

A thousand beats of my heart
A thousand tears pool
like raindrops into lifeless puddles
laying dormant on a deserted highway

A thousand memories illuminate my mind
A thousand kisses warm my soul
like an unusual guest arriving unexpectedly
at the bed and breakfast of my day

A thousand nervous bumps upon my skin
A thousand dreams wrap around me
like a warm body against the winter chill
permeating this moment

A thousand jumbled messages scramble for first place
A thousand words unwritten remain
like a ghost haunting me
until exorcised upon the page

A thousand moments peering from the pool of my coffee
A thousand questions harmonising
like a rehearsal of the unsung chorus
in the musical yet scored

A thousand pages of a poet's verse
A thousand melodies and lyrics lilt nearby
A thousand shades of colour thrust upon my canvas
Guide me home

Until next we meet:

"May your evenings fade and your mornings begin with a soft breeze gifting a gentle kiss, bringing tingles upon your skin and leaving butterfly footprints upon your heart."

A NOTE OF THANKS

Thank you for joining me in this second collection;
may it bring you continuous enjoyment.

Namaste,

Dianne

CPSIA information can be obtained
at www.ICGtesting.com
Printed in the USA
BVHW051356080321
601998BV00011BA/1199